BITTEN HAIR

First published in 2019 by Blue Diode Press
Reprinted, 2020

30 Lochend Road
Leith
Edinburgh EH6 8BS
www.bluediode.co.uk

ISBN: 978-1-9164051-1-0

Typesetting: Rob A. Mackenzie.
text in Minion Pro, 11 pt

Cover art: 'Choreography' by Tessa Berring
Cover design and typography: Gerry Cambridge

Diode logo design: Sam and Ian Alexander.

Printed and bound by Imprint Digital, Exeter, UK.
https://digital.imprint.co.uk

BITTEN HAIR

Tessa Berring

Blue Diode Press
Edinburgh

Contents

for my family

Illustration

The first thing I did
to the figure
was lightly
remove its head

Embrace Me

Skin is wipe-clean
and my jeans fit well

and once I wrote

about my dream
with men in it –

all cotton wool heads!

I chopped them off
of course

which was bloody
like tampons

and my hands stank
of dead petunia

It was a good story
nuanced and delicate

someone said

though they might not
have meant it

It's a relief about skin
being easy to wipe

and it's good having jeans
all over my legs

I like lean words,
you know, like 'spirit'

and lightly placed
unspeakable things

Playing House

I'd like a golden apple
or a red one, or I'll cry

(This room is so tiny
when covered in snow)

Did you hear about the woman
who bound her face

in hot spun sugar
as a protest against everything?

We could do things too
like breathing in, then out

Oh my God, oh my God
you'd really love that, wouldn't you?

A Raindrop

reveals itself
by dropping

solidarity
is an emotion

feet are powerful

being alive is
and tabby cats

find me a ghost
to rock with

and lavender

I am warm as froth
and language is froth

Some Things Are Meant to Be

Someone was singing
with low notes and long vowels

a love song

how lovely of course
(heart heart heart heart)

I wanted to make
all my friends listen

then tell them that
I am not at all in love

I'd try to imagine
one of them saying

'oh I could fall for you
you wondrous buttery creature'

to which I'd repeat 'buttery?'
and not with a throaty growl

Bandit

There's not a thing
you need to hear, oh bandit

like whether day
is closer than night

whether shelves will stay up
or drop from a wall

made of yellow ironed paper

No one mentions
the room with the elephant

the woman with a nickname
the much less of me

'Everything begins and ends
at exactly the right time and place'

says the guide

Is this true?
And shall we spend the night together?

Talk of sad love
or those tiny egg-ish daisies

is how to woo me completely
I'm afraid

Don't Buy Slippers, Buy a Little Knife

1.

These cyclamen spots

Do I look as if I don't
eat properly?

It's how things are after all

Ice cream
Precision instruments

Only of afterwards
that's what I'm afraid of

You come through
or you don't

A tiny drop of coffee

2.

I love your dress
Thanks, it stains

Would you like some rice?
Several redcurrants?

Sometimes I lie down in cars
to be bitten

but I do like rice
plus clouds in springtime

Soap is quite the thing
isn't it?

Legs in the bathtub
turning it pink

Look

it's all for the image –
how a thing just *is*

the shape, the sound
the cut, the edge

the 'uh oh!'

the cow and the clouds
are not pretty

oh yes they are pretty
oh no they're not

and so it becomes
a pantomime

all the time

and the news is bad
all the time

the news is on
while we eat the veg

and are attracted

(sometimes at least
we are attracted)

to each other

wear what you like
and cherish the future

it is never behind you –
uh oh, it is

Quiz

1.

(She slops her thighs in the sorry little moat
and longs to be a dappled carp
But God gave her legs
like soft heavy scissors…)

I am finding things to talk about
like fish and scissors and my legs

Once I did a quiz:

What is your favourite part of your body?

My legs

You are ready for anything!

I don't know why I said legs
I don't know why…

2.

But I didn't run
he told me not to

What would you do with lots of money?

I would squeak
I would turn myself into a squeaky toy

I would turn myself into
a gingerbread woman
taunt people with spices
and stale body parts

Or I could sit down
and paint apple cores
with white enamel paint
glue frogs to motorbikes
line a drawer with little pills

What a question!

Flight

Is the god dead? I don't know
Are you young? Very young

Lemons turn soft
in the microwave

Lemons from the trees
where all the swallows

Furniture

If there were more jokes there'd be more jackdaws
What time do you call this? (asks someone)
Call it another day, call it a pussy cat
call it a soft bound atlas
of the world

Painting

It's November and damp, like the time you flew
somewhere, and the sky seemed petrified for weeks

I found a woman with abstract hands and yellow cheeks
who said, 'philosophy is no consolation for bitten hair'

I'll always be glad I pulled the rotting plum from the tree
how the branch lifted into the leaves, altering an image

Dreams Are Made with Vanishing in Mind

Apples won't juice
in my electric blender

I go swimming whenever I like though
and I'm a little afraid of dying

I have my reasons:

hair falling out
and nearby bread knives

Cotton wool is perfect
for soft daubs

and for wrapping
my small glass octopus

Have you noticed the way
a horizon seesaws?

How the stench of bruised fruit
could well be something else?

Sugar

What they said was that I need
to take it seriously, that eels should
be bought alive, that when I imitate

a prehistoric creature I must immerse
myself in the idea completely, and not
treat it as a kind of play acting

I find it hard though, to get down on all fours,
to grunt and paw the ground
without laughing

Buy your eels alive, they said, so I do
Their bodies are strong
I like to think they love me (they don't love me)

I wear mohair jumpers covered in ribbons
I wear denim gloves which people compliment
for the tight pink stitching and studs

The Blue Leotard

was tight, so tight
it scored her thighs

in blood electric rings

neither cornflower
nor forget-me-not

she walks across the floor

stiff as a basin
collecting rain

What They Said

The power said, *so this is what opposite feels like*

The specific bruise said, *I don't remember how it happened*

The lover said, *I whistle in the dark*

The motorway said, *the world is not in the middle*

The stranger said, *my tongue has been disqualified*

The truth said, *I suppose an owl still hoots?*

The landscape said, *ugliness is the wrong perspective*

The rose-hip said, *I am nothing but a wound*

The window said, *so this is what pleasure looks like*

Arcadia said, *run as fast as you can!*

The wardrobe said, *it is so completely quiet*

The pronoun said, *the silence is on fire*

Idea For Persimmons

To run barefoot
downstairs

still drizzled
with sex or soap

to quarter persimmons
and start to chew

Whole Bloody Endeavour

1.

I could live on oranges if that would work
but last night I was a rubber ball, and a star said

I bet you bought face cream last year
which is correct – lots and lots of face cream!

Please don't be bored by my jokes about the snow
(everything starts dripping when the sun comes out)

I keep sentences in vases, they last around three days
feathers are not so-so they are perfect

2.

(feathers are not so so they are perfect

even dishevelled
they are perfect
even all wet

what am I saying?
what do I know about perfection
about feathers
about all wet

god nothing
I am making it all up
all of it

don't leave!
please wait!

feathers are so muscular

and on ducks
and on pigeons
and on pelicans
and wrens
and that Papua New Guinea wonder bird
the cassowary)

An Intention to Be Present

I bought a bathmat
on Sunday morning

the equivalent

of not worshipping God
at exactly the same time

I needed to soap myself

to peel things off
and not slip over

I love the way Veronica
puts on lip salve

in the movie
about her double life

and I certainly know
what dew is

and how wetness
slides around a hand

The bathmat is off white
almost grey

a bit like something
to feel sad about

something to kneel down on
perhaps pray

Prayer

I want to make some money
wear lace if I have to

The butter was left out again
and I can't bear to watch people

wrestling on beaches

when I want people to leave
I tell them I am going to sleep

and start making understatements
about melancholia

Sometimes I might have meat to cook
which can't wait

I want people to stop
sending me photographs

They remind me of how peculiar mouths are

I'm a damp expanse, like a halibut
only halibut means 'sacred' and 'flat'

Paste

She used to say indoor snails
taste of marzipan

and her nipples
taste of marzipan

and her tongue and
the small of her back

She used to say this
because she longed to be

an almond, a huge hollow almond
full of upright Madonnas

all praying for love
and unimaginable purity

Cafe

So I find myself explaining
that I am sexually languorous

(as in not sexually voracious)

I explain it with a degree of optimism
but god, I'm lazy

and unskilled in excitement

Next to me on a window sill
is a thigh-high statue of a hare

pointing a rifle at a yucca plant

My mind goes blank for a moment –
this used to be an opticians!

The reality is that nobody listens
so I put back the water jug and pen

Shade

and the beach is suddenly liquid

Or the red table that was always
so heavy

with vodka, vodka
skin and graffiti

It is terribly hot
and there are no more messages

mint slabs, deep cuts

No one sleeps in this house –

sex and broken necklaces
that's what I mean

Sometimes the sky
is all I can think about

or bitten hair

or lipstick that does nothing
but a pale smear

August

The air spat
and I spit

and don't sleep
for heat

or a need to walk
uphill

and not suffer

make it still!

Kisses add saliva
to objects

all those movable lips

plus black grapes
plus green grapes

tasting of soap

She Wants Real Sea

She is very normal looking
and she often peels a grape

to yell, 'look at my wet eyeball!'
She can also be monumental

and smells good in a sheet
Forgiveness tastes

like sunlit sand dunes
says the cheerful book

but she knows better
Forgiveness tastes of thighs

and a spat out picnic
People turn her on

like a monophonic radio –
'it's ok, oh its ok'

She longs to slice a line
through thin blue canvas

She cannot be anybody's
mother today

Chairs

This box has five pairs
of scissors in it

I must not lose them
on a journey

I don't believe in

There is a yellow rainbow
that can never be a chimney

and an ordinary boy
is missing

Not a ghost
he is a little bit pirate

This room is so soft
I could cut it

down the middle
five or seven times

Chairs can be such
solemn objects

am I crying?
Somebody once said

'be jollier
be like a warm lap'

I'll never forget that

Shock

The floor is drenched in green disinfectant
The monkey is limp, blue, decapitated

Come and examine my grid!

I use it to mark gradations of red
from pink through blush to scarlet

It is utterly harmless

like listening to string partitas
is harmless

when you no longer talk to your pet

I used to talk to cats
(miaow, miaow, miaow)

but not any more

I greet them in silence
as if they are furred spectres

with no language I can share, idiot!

The monkey is limp, blue…
did I mention that?

Or that all I ask for
is an expression of grace

and that you come to me
when I am recumbent

and comfortable, my electric friend,
before colour fades as it always fades:

amaranth, sunset, peppercorn
raspberry, hellebore, blood

Women

who don't know gentleness
long to make blancmange

to tip it down the necks
of comfortable funnels

whispering words like
buttocks and fandango

Flag

The body would like a gorgeous lemon drink
It would like to go out for just a teeny tiny walk
and not be found
wanting

Home Ec.

knives aren't soft
but snow is soft

hyacinths are real
and lips are soft

a moth is soft
saliva is soft

putty is hard
nasturtiums, soft

stains are brown
oranges are real

words aren't bubbles
bubbles are soft

cuts are red
sheets are soft

love isn't hard
love isn't soft

Apple Core

When he fucks her
she feels

like an apple core

an apple core
or a snail

knotted in its shell

at least, this is how
it used to be

until she discovered

that tickling the back
of the air

with her cold pink toes
was funny

she can pretend to
be wearing stilts

but upside down

Embrace Me II

I'm not good enough good enough
are you good enough

for sex in a dream?

it happened last night
and there was bright red jelly

I wasn't going to tell you
as the image is just mine, but

small, moulded, bright red jellies
the shape of peppers

with the stalk sliced off

it's a thrill to write quickly
and it's good to keep in mind

bodies are wet tissues
plus air, some bones, some puke

sometimes what I'd love
is to put an end to poems

I also need a cough drop
and to climb steep hills with you

we might get out of breath
but we'll wear our nicest clothes

my orange wool-mix coat
with the brown buckle belt

your raw silk off-white blouse
and wide leg trousers

Vagueness

Like whether there are shadows
or a space

between the words

blouse, gnat, grip, core, lint, jelly, lulla-lulla

hey! does anyone know what wax smells of?
(digestive systems? paper hats?)

it took forever to think of ferris-wheel
for the crossword

nothing else fit

not even helter-skelter
which could have been perfect

The idea of a quilted beast
is poetic

lukewarm snow is water

because I opened the screw top bottle
they said *you've got great hands!*

everything can always be another thing

is that consoling?

Some Refreshment Is Good

The sun is too bright for this
(hair dryer, hair dryer)

Why make everything so damn beautiful?
Why make everything about

'loving you still when I mustn't?'

I need prawn shells and wet leaves
emeralds and banana trees and orange trees

or lemon trees

tails on the ends of animals

or morning stars and evening stars
or evening dress and morning dress

black and blue and black and blue
whoever you are, whoever you are

(slower, more tender)

whoever you are, whoever you are

An Appetite

Call me
a locust, slowly

and repetitively
I won't mind!

One time I believed
I might actually

shed my skin –
but I only hurt

and we had
to stop pulling

I've changed though
people tell me

for better or
for worst

Small Talk, Say, Flies

It's basically longing, that is all (laughter) (laughter?)
The computers full of people and pieces of people

And people far away with their pretty brushed ponies
(That nobody rides, thank God!)

Stick flowers where it hurts – Oleander, Tulips
Or stick them in your hair and take one hundred photographs

Whole hay bales in your hair, and take one hundred photographs
Botany wins the language game far too easily

And certain seats are red if you need to bleed discreetly

◉

It's basically that we don't want it to end
And we know we don't want it to end

So we stand in our sewn clothes and laugh out loud
About how near death is, how near nothing is

Despite waltzing on a stage in turquoise light
Despite meat and anemones and gas-lit routes through a park

I'd like to brush my teeth, a clean routine activity
Please wait at the reception desk – the foyer has a stag in it

('The foyer has a stag in it?' is what you're bound to say)

Window

And no time at all
to wonder whether or not

a distinction between skin
and the flame out there

yes flames and the skin
or long brushed hair

and float our impeccable voices

TWO SEQUENCES

Shift

Things take place, wax and street lights take place, a space-blue water pipe, a dance shuffle, trace smell submersion of things, one eye open or mollusc hand squeeze, today a thing takes place, a shock of hidden (that songbird!), or honeycomb art place, whirr whirr thumb propeller takes place, peel soft nothing takes place, waste mould anemone, icicle, or rose leaf.

A sudden shift
to the varnish
on a terracotta peach,
to the noiseless up and down
of brand new elevators
to a garden of plastic magnolias
and the possibility that the sun
might rain how a cloud rains.

A click clack of high heels
crosses a beeswaxed floor
to lines etched on a wall
and a razor slicing through
pomegranate. It deserves
mention – the glisten of seeds,
the slope of the spirit level,
juice flying as it happened.

Beneath the furniture – look!
a prone woman thinks
about the difference
between the surface of a pond
and the surface of a table;
about the way lead flickers,
peppermints dissolve,
and dreams are always free.

The stage is covered in
criss-cross Sellotape,
an idea is looking
for needles and a saw.
(There is more to this
than meets the eye).
The dancer exits left,
the canary pecks
the bars of its cage
which sparks, then explodes.

Inside the pillar is molten fog,
behind the pillar is an apple,
before the pillar is the origin
of the pillar. Beneath the ice
cube is a tiny cold pond.

Where is the vending machine?
Where is the kiss?
Chemistry is delicate
where is the artist?
Oh absence, oh presence,
oh cheap polythene
covering an exhibit with creases.

Red and orange tones are correct for this layer;
overhead, helicopters make flying sounds.
Try something once with no sense of bliss,
a second time with absolute bliss.
The 'coo coo' of pigeons is difficult to imitate;
the far edge of the page is where to lay your glove.

T is for catastrophe, P for mutability,
L for upholstery, why not?
Add bodies, trolleys, goggles, sci-fi.
Go sideways with the spatula,
pin up the draught, let trees sleep
and wisteria spread everywhere.

An unknown known by the scenic route;
working with peeled eyes and tweezers
for every microscopic surprise.
And who got the furnace in the lucky dip?
Who got the squirrel, the pressed periwinkle?

The Most Emotional Woman

*after a painting by Paul Klee, 'Portrait of an
Emotional Woman', sometimes translated from
the German as 'Emotional Portrait of a Woman'*

1.

I am a most emotional woman
drinking coffee in a tight fitting dress.
On the table is an apple and
a painted triangle. By morning light
the triangle appears blue
by evening light, deep aubergine.

2.

I am a most emotional woman
who finds ghosts on the handles
of my saucepans. Who finds ghosts
on the handles of her saucepans?
I do. What uneasy thoughts they
give me! I wash my hair to forget
the shapes of their mouths, I turn on
a weather forecast for somewhere
in the North Pacific.

3.

I am a most emotional woman
who loves the proximity
of unfurnished rooms full of nothing
but white sheets and winged heroines.
There might be an upturned colander,
an engraving of a pear tree, or words
such as *'promise me one thing,*
just one thing'.

4.

I am a most emotional woman
who conceives of things ironically.
Things like self portraits, dinner,
sometimes sex, never wretchedness.

5.

I am a most emotional woman
and I no longer look at anyone.
There are cigarettes and rose-hips
crushed onto the pavement.
A foundation can give way at any
moment.

6.

I am a most emotional woman;
how insistent I am, how swollen.
Lock me in a house where
I can listen to the flight
of hawk moths, dress up
in my own shadows,
put my arms around my own
shoulders, keep marigolds
on a windowsill.

7.

I am a most emotional woman
and marigolds sound so very
charming. 'Choose us!' shout the
marigolds (if marigolds were ever
to shout, if marigolds were ever
to metamorphose into wireless
radio-phones or loud mouthed
narcissists).

8.

I am a most emotional woman
and miracles don't work.
There are strict rules and no
new angels, only nose diving
aeroplanes and different
degrees of magnetism.

9.

I am a most emotional woman
and this is my dramatic performance.
What do you think? It is more
than a little comedy strip, but less
than a battlefield, where even
living things are not alive.

10.

I am a most emotional woman
who loves snails and abstract
memories. I place exotic
objects on the carpet. Exotic
objects like printed bed clothes
and soft men, coffee pots decorated
with green enamel sun-loungers,
the teeth from some sacrificial bull.

11.

I am a most emotional woman
who needs to move quickly
or I will be called on to make
conversation, when all I have
to talk about is a red brick
bungalow opposite a red brick
museum, where I once saw
a collar dove break its neck.

12.

I am a most emotional woman
so I know about screaming
and unfinished metamorphosis;
the egg that never cracks,
the mask that never comes off,
the people of the future that
never stop their fearful dancing.

13.

I am a most emotional woman
and find emptiness enchanting.
The empty tangerine, the empty
satsuma, the empty pomegranate.
The empty space between one
world and the other that can
barely be filled with sleep.

14.

I am a most emotional woman
biting into a red apple as if
it is filled with explosive.
Boum! Boum! Boum! Boum!
Look carefully around the room,
are there any walls left?
Whatever the answer, *mon amour*,
lets sleep like logs tonight.

15.

I am a most emotional woman,
and believe this is not enough.
It has to be sweeter or more sour
or more like when I lie down
and no one notices I am wearing
nothing but pink feathers, the exact
same pink as Germoline or Silvo,
stitched together like two rattlesnakes.

16.

I am a most emotional woman.
Beginnings are the quietest place.
Shh. Lets go. Back to the beginning,
back to the before. 'Too-wit, too-wit'
said the owl, 'tick tick' said the clock.
Have we bricks? A blanket? A table
lamp? Are there magazines to roll
into soft telescopes to imagine
the sky is magnified?

The Surgery is Filled with Female Poets

after a poem by Anne-Laure Coxam

Hello everyone!
Wow, what are the chances?
We're all here!
I enjoyed your book
Me too
And yours
And yours
What a lot of books there are
So many
Exciting times!
What are you doing here?
And you?
I have a pain there
And there
Smear
Me too
Living on the edge
You know
Shit
Sad
Pills
My vagina buzzes
Seems to
Or a dull ache
Did you ever read that book?
I prefer the buzz thing
Definitely
Like too much coffee
Exciting times!
Everyone wants to be queen
I mean…

How long can nostalgia last?
It doesn't even taste good
Who said cherries?
It was her idea
She looked like a mermaid
Beautiful
But with legs
We should meet for coffee more
There and there
It buzzes?
Hums inside
Probably nothing
Good to see the doctor
To get out
Read the newspapers
Did you see?
I know, like exile
Want to say more really
The pain is too much
Never enough words
Or the right language
Even for female poets!
We're in the right place
For now
Seriously
Lets meet up soon
When we feel better
There'll be more books
Yours?
Yours?
Hope you sort it

There and there
Whatever it is
I agree
This dull ache
It buzzes
I agree but
Buzz is
The wrong word

ACKNOWLEDGEMENTS

Thanks to the editors of the following journals and anthologies where some of these poems first appeared:

Adjacent Pineapple, Coup de Teatre (Summerhall Galleries, 2016), Datableedzine, Duet Duet (Pity Milk Press), Gutter, Magma Poetry, Makar/UnMakar: Twelve Contemporary Poets in Scotland (Tapsalteerie, 2019), Mote, The Rialto, Smithereens Press, South Bank Poetry, Spark (Blue Diode Press, 2018), Women on the Road (Fruitmarket Gallery, 2018).

I Am a Most Emotional Woman was performed at the StAnza International Poetry Festival in 2016.

Some poems in this collection emerged through writing and performing with the poetry collective '12'

Tessa Berring's pamphlet *Cut Glass and No Flowers* was published by Dancing Girl Press in 2017. In addition to her own writing, she engages regularly with other collaborative and interdisciplinary art projects. She also works extensively in translation, most recently in Riga, with the Latvian Literature Platform. *Bitten Hair* is her first full collection.